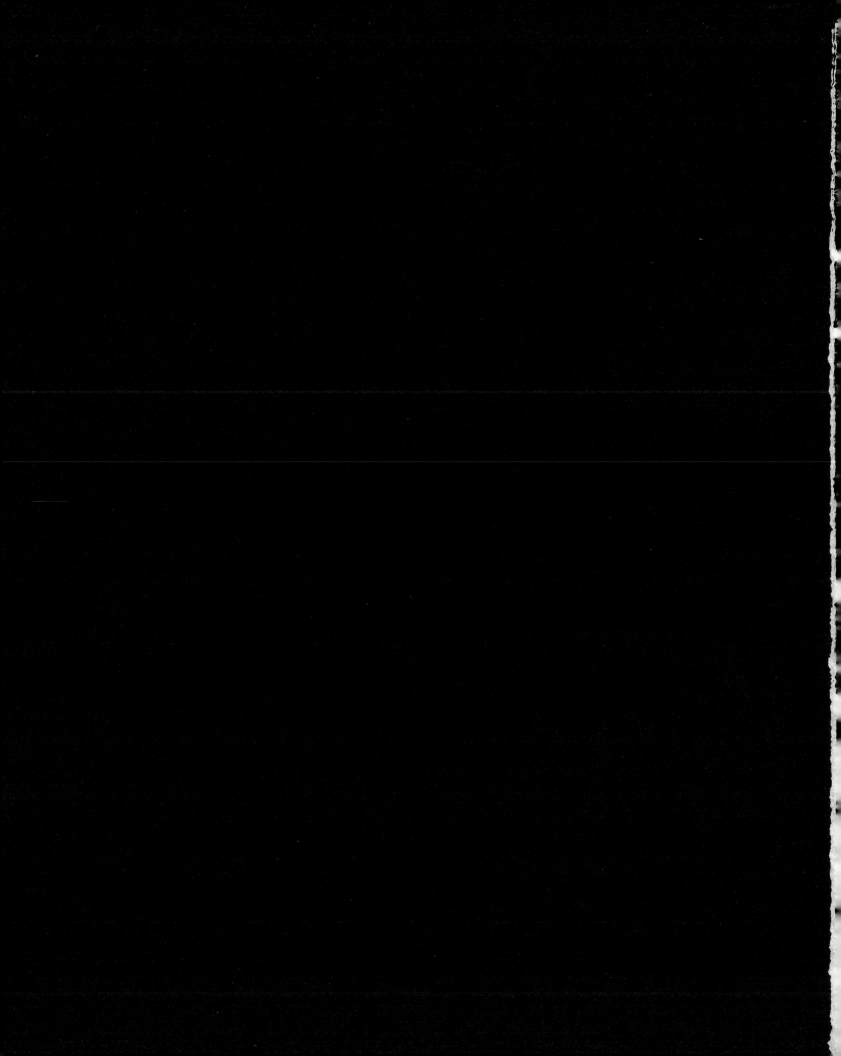

"COLOUR IS COMMUNICATION"

*Published with the generous
support from:*

The Politiken Foundation
The New Carlsberg Foundation
The Beckett Foundation
The Oticon Foundation

Thanks to:

Norman Foster
Spencer de Grey
Joe Hainal
Christian Hallmann
Katy Harris
Peter Hiort
David Jenkins
Thomas Manns
David Nelson
Graham Phillips
David Rosenberg
John Small
Carsten Thau

PER **ARNOLDI**
"COLOUR IS COMMUNICATION" SELECTED PROJECTS FOR **FOSTER**+PARTNERS
1996 > 2006

To Jean-François Decaux who saw it first.

BIRKHÄUSER – PUBLISHERS FOR ARCHITECTURE   BASEL · BOSTON · BERLIN

CONTENTS

Trying to characterise Per Arnoldi evokes many responses. Colourful – in all kinds of ways. Resourceful – always quick to sense an elegant solution. Witty – a constant fund of anecdotes and insights. Succinct – the master of the poster-sized one-liner. He is, of course, all these things, and that is what has made him such a pleasure and inspiration to work with over the years.

My colleagues and I have involved Per in many projects in the past, beginning with the Commerzbank in Frankfurt and the Reichstag in Berlin, and continuing with the Police Memorial and a family of projects for Imperial College, all in London.

Too often, perhaps, as architects, we are hypnotised by white, silver and grey. Per has helped us to add a splash of colour to our palette. For me, the most successful collaborations with Per have also had a strategic component. In each case, adding colour has brought our thinking into sharper focus. The Commerzbank illustrates this perfectly. By colour-coding the circulation cores in Per's signature primaries of red, yellow and blue we were able to make the experience of navigating the building simple and pleasurable. The broad-brush colour scheme of the lift lobbies is continued in the fine detail of the building's signage systems, which Per also devised, so that you are guided from the lobby

08 to your office by the simple expedient of following your designated colour. It sounds simple, but like writing a short letter, a simple idea often requires a huge amount of work before you achieve the required result.

This book details twenty-five projects that Per has contributed to, or devised with us, over the years – from graphic design and posters to works of art and colour schemes. It is a rich and diverse body of work – an accurate reflection, I think, of Per's incredible breadth of interest and quickness of mind.

Per Arnoldi and Norman Foster
Commerzbank 18. July 1997

WHO'S AFRAID OF RED, YELLOW AND BLUE by PER ARNOLDI

The story begins here. Or rather in Copenhagen fifteen years ago. And in New York shortly afterwards. The French street furniture company JCDecaux was tussling with the problem of introducing advertising columns, bus stops and all their other bits of street furniture in Copenhagen. The city needed a new inventory, but recognised with icey, cocksure, dismissive provincial arrogance, how something like this had to be done here in Designland.
And so a competition for a series of new bus stops was held.
And won, quite rightly, by the able Danish architect Knud Holscher.
A prototype was set up on City Hall Square but was then allowed to fall into disrepair.
That's how a winner looks!
Or rather that is how even a bright and shiny winner looked – sad, smashed, graffiti-infested, dirty and unusable – after a very short while, without maintenance, here in Designland.

JCDecaux did not give up, but pointed out, as firmly as possible, that it could be done better. Even in Designland!

Contact was established and the city hall people visited JCDecaux's shiny, polished, perfect headquarters and exhibition area at Versailles. At that time I had just designed a poster for Copenhagen, Clean City, primarily built up around a question mark that simply and effectively examined the lack of cleaning and maintenance in the dirty old city. A self-critical advertisement, to give the city its due.

Copenhagen's city engineer sent this poster to JCDecaux who registered this Danish visitation with their usual tremendous efficiency by installing it in all the pillars, pots and stops exhibited in their show street.
Among them, illuminated at night, was Foster + Partners poster column – an icon of optimistic modernism.

And soon afterwards when they wanted to try setting up a couple of Foster's street furniture designs in New York, they asked me to design a poster for the city and for Foster's fantastic advertising column.

Contact with J C Decaux and Norman Foster was established and Jean-François Decaux saw more potential here – as he always does.

That is what this book is about.

It all hangs together, if you are lucky.

Incidentally, Holscher's design won, on Decaux's initiative, and became a reality.
I was introduced to Norman Foster at his office in

12 London and nothing was ever the same again.
So far so good.

2

Luis Barragán knew and showed that a colour
can only become both one colour and all colours
when the light is right.
From the dark tube of the corridor, the faraway
end wall glows at us, lit by the patterns of day and
night through the side window.
All cats are fair in the dark.
And in the faintest light, colour smoulders,
gathering to pounce. The colours of the walls
should not be displayed, but allowed to live
their own diurnal life, in which it may be early
morning or late twilight that produces the most
beautiful colour.

Wrapped in receding darkness, colour comes
to life. On the way into the gathering darkness of
evening it glows with the day's last, warm,
saved-up embers of light.

On a shelf in his own house stands a gold-leaf
image by the artist Mathias Goeritz.
An unorthodox icon.
A piece of non-architecture gives away the true
secret of gold: it glows!
A single accent with a continent's dramatic and
tragic history within it.

From the warm green water off the coast in Cancún
I see the deep Barragánian pink of the hotel
trembling and shimmering against the intense,
deep blue of the Mexican sky.
Only here, in this place, in this light, at this time
can that colour work.

It would not do in London.
A colour is never alone.
The eye, too, remembers where it is.

3

One evening in 1961 while Yuri Gagarin orbited
space as the first human being to see Earth from
out there, he exclaimed, 'It's blue!' Yves Klein
was in Paris that evening at a private party,
listening to Gagarin on the radio.
When the exclamation 'It's blue' came – out of the
blue and into the space from outer space – Klein
said: 'I knew it!'

Klein's own desperate, emotional and very moving
attempt to fly – 'Je me jète dans la vide' – shows
the way.

With its matte surface, Klein's radiant, pure,
ultramarine blue pigment swallows the light.
The picture opens inwards.
His witty and very astute comment on that come-
dancing contest couple, Art + Money, where he

transmutes blue into gold and fixes it in gold-leaf
pictures, lets the light move the opposite way.
The gold glitters and glows.
We still have that option.
Shut out the light with the matte surface, wrap a
colour in a vortex of infinity, or let the colour,
the surface, gloss or gold, shine out into the space
we have available.
Not Gagarin's space. Foster's space.

4

'Colour is communication, don't you agree?' was
the first sentence Norman spoke in 1995 when he
called me from London to invite me to work
with him on the design of the Commerzbank in
Frankfurt.
An invitation to a dance that was to be more
wide-ranging and complicated than I had ever
tried before; which was longer and harder
and – best of all – would force me to revise so
many of the practices that had borne me up
through mainstream abstract painting for many
years and helped me to find solutions for a
number of visually very direct poster commissions.
Yes, I agree, colours tell a story, and yes, I had
practiced articulating and fine-tuning this story,
but not in that order of magnitude, not within
that hard-nosed, relentlessly necessary logistical
framework, and not in the lowness and loftiness
of real life.

And yes, we can communicate with colour but
it is essential to understand and accept that colour
does not communicate at all.
Only in context!!!

Colours in themselves carry no story. Colours in
themselves mean nothing. Colours are not words.

But colours, as we were so painfully reminded
by the client at the presentation of our first designs
for the Commerzbank, can be bearers in context
of a conventional meaning, a code, from which the
innocent and quite unoffending colour can have
a hard job breaking free.

For example:
Red in itself does not mean love.
Nor black grief.
Nor green hope.
Nor yellow optimism.

In the Commerzbank context, green meant the
Dresden Bank, red meant the Socialists (who they
perhaps were not so sweet on), blue meant Deutsche
Bank, and, luckily, yellow meant Commerzbank.

In the Reichstag building in Berlin, out next big job,
green meant the Greens (not the Dresden Bank),
black meant the Fascists, red the Reds (not love at
all) and blue the Conservatives.
Quod erat demonstrandum.

14 Colours can be ascribed and coded with a symbolic value which you accept in a certain cultural context – accept and must submit to if you are the one who has to shift the colours into place.

UNLESS you can set the colours free.

Unless you can detach the poor colours from all codes and start from scratch!

This was the exercise, and for many years now this has been the true exercise in every colour-scheme job. First, to set the colours free.
Then, to define the job, and finally, to get the free, unencumbered, virgin colours properly into play!

For the same reason I do not believe in colour psychology.
The endless mumbo-jumbo of the women's magazines is nothing but entertainment.

But I believe in the articulation of colours in every man-made context (for good reasons we cannot do anything about nature – that is probably why we are killing it off). I believe in the experience of this articulation.

I believe that without prior assumptions, without training, with no knowledge of codes, we can feel whether a colour in a context in a piece of architecture or in a picture or a city has been added and incorporated beneficially.
Because somebody wishes you well.

I suppose that that is the real modernist credo.
That it can work.
That it can be done properly.
And that it therefore must be done properly.
The experience of articulated freedom must be our goal.

I wonder if that is what Norman meant when he called in 1995.
In all events, this is what we have done.

Painting has been declared dead again and again and survived every time.
In 1921, in one masterly stroke , Alexander Rodchenko declared painting finally dead with his three canvases:
Pure Red Color (Chistyi krasnyi tsvet), Pure Yellow Color (Chistyi zheltyi tsvet) Pure Blue Color (Chistyi sinii tsvet) 1921,
These colours, he stated, marked the final point in the long colourful history of painting.
But it was at the same time a point of departure into a bright, free, just and shining future, where the same colours would, I guess, reappear brighter than ever.

At least it has been for us.

'You're on your way into one of modernism's
erogenous zones,' the architecture professor
Carsten Thau told me in a live radio discussion on
the modern picture/world-picture from the
Louisiana Museum of Modern Art north of Copenhagen.
I had raised the issue of the meaning of the detail
in Mondrian's black grid. That it had in fact not
been painted right out to the edge of the canvas,
and had actually not managed to touch the end
of the painting.
I do not think we got any closer to the answer, but
then I suppose it is like that with erogenous zones:
if and when you get too close to them, not only
do all grids stop, but all rationality, and the senses
take over.
Mondrian's studio in Paris from 1921 to 1936
is probably the erogenous temple par excellence
if you happen to be preoccupied with the eternal
exercise: how is the order of colours to be
experienced as order, and when should all order
yield to the wanton voluptuousness and juicy
sensuality of colours?

'God is in the detail,' Mies van der Rohe said, and
the rest of us have repeated it all too often.

'Death is in the detail,' Norman grumbled one
afternoon in Frankfurt, where the encounter of an

indoor, free-standing stair cylinder with floor and
carpet suddenly would not offer any meaningful
solution, and the whole office's impressive
machinery ground to a halt.
Recess or panel or nothing. Out or in or straight
down?

The edge of the picture, the grim abyss, threatened.
Had we lost the focus and failed to see the picture
for the frame, or were we still on the track of
the eroticism we thought could be coaxed out even
from a detail on the 48th (management) floor?

I was there for the sake of the carpet colour, and
four paintings, but precisely this – possibly small
– shadow was important.

Could the drawing in the room bear the sudden
appearance of a black contour?

And when is the unfinished a finish in its own right,
and acceptable?

When does the blue carpet stop being blue and
become a thing with a shaggy edge?

When the only thing the self-imposed rules
absolutely dictate is that it cannot not matter?

Mondrian patiently moved his colour fields up and
down and back and forth in his little space.

16 It is never either just 'it'll do' or 'it doesn't matter'; the exercise itself, the hunt for the magic moment when the elements fall into place and you recognise a suggestion as just right – although you have never seen it before – becomes an obsession.

6

One late afternoon in April, my British Airways plane from Copenhagen was forced to circle a few times in the low sun over London in preparation for landing.
The view from this looping tour was incredible.
The traces of Foster + Partners in London were clearly visible.
There, the giant arch of Wembley Stadium; there, Swiss Re's heaven-pointing rocket shape in the City; there, the GLA's new, spacey mayor's offices at Tower Bridge and the slim bridge across the Thames in front of Tate Modern.

Here, a little closer to Heathrow, JCDecaux headquarters' extension to one of the Great West Road's classic Deco buildings; here the design office and Norman's green penthouse and the sun-gold wave form of the Albion.
And then, surprisingly clear from up here in the sky, the whole Imperial College Campus between the Royal Albert Hall and the Natural History Museum.
The Faculty Building – at eye level, hidden away in an inner courtyard from where the blue block of the building hits you like a blow as you first arrive, but from way up here visible as a blue sacred monolith amidst a sea of Kensington sand-stone, visible again and again and again, several times all the way round.

The three blue shades which now, in the late sun and sharp shadow, shift from warm to cold to a thousand variations and resolute monochrome, stand there as an image of the office's mantra (as I have experienced it):
FOCUS!
A dash of colour. A brilliant metonym for Foster's constant endeavours – focus and context:
No form is just art.
No colour exists for its own sake.
No structure is sufficient unto itself.
No smart inventiveness is worth the bother.
Everything must be seen and understood and defined and articulated within the context in which it is to appear.
Only then does all form produce meaning, and all colours become communication.

Only then can we land.

PA: "Grey _is_ a colour..."

NF: "You start to sound like me... !

Norman Foster to Per Arnoldi, London 15.11.2005

Commerzbank
Frankfurt, 1997

Colour Concept
Signage
Paintings

19

20 How lucky can you get?

If you've quite got over Barnett Newman's very direct question "Who is afraid of red, yellow, and blue?" and are not afraid of red, yellow, and blue and have understood Mondrian's demonstration of the endless spatial possibilities of the interplay and overlap of these three colours, and do not see Rodchenko's three ultimate canvases from 1921 as a threatening blind alley, but as an open door and an open invitation to the dance, or simply to a new music, you are lucky.

If you are then invited to create a colour scheme for a new building in Frankfurt that consists of three towers where the traffic pattern plays this exact melody with three overlapping, intersecting routes that have to be kept apart and lead into and up to one another without getting lost, you are very, very lucky.

It was the Commerzbank whose at once alluringly simple and sophisticatedly complex structures Foster's patient co-workers began to drum into my head in 1995.

The construction site was a multilingual Babel of a deep black hole in the ground, but it was already high time to lay down a strategy for the towers that would shoot up from the hole.

They manhandled the concrete and the logistics, and I grappled with a plan for the colours. Who's afraid of red, yellow, and blue? Well, the client was, for, as I've pointed out before, we hadn't primed the pump for our optimistic primarycoloured presentation and ran, headlong and smiling, into a wall of conventional interpretations of the suggested colours.

"Find some other colours" was the laconic message I got from the client to work on with.

"I don't have any other colours" wasn't an answer that would have encouraged further collaboration, so we kept a very low profile until the building began to rise, and we thought the tangible design of traffic routes and the divisions of the building would support our logic.

In 1:1, a very risky scale if you really are on the wrong track, we mocked up exactly the signposting which in red (five reds too), yellow (or rather five yellows), and five blues made up our slightly more refined second proposition for the design of the signals that would support everyday traffic and orientation in the building.

It was a success.

"Das ist ja aber logisch," was the equally laconic blessing upon our interpretation of the building, on our very simple choice of colours.

The logic eliminated the conventions...or rather introduced new conventions for the reading of the fundamentally innocuous colours. The building had taken on a life of its own.

Then the job took off and grew, with all the signposting, a huge steel door, and four large paintings for the management floor.

In red and yellow and blue.

7·19·35·36-50

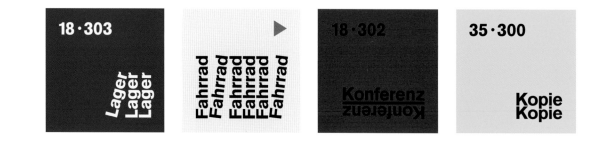

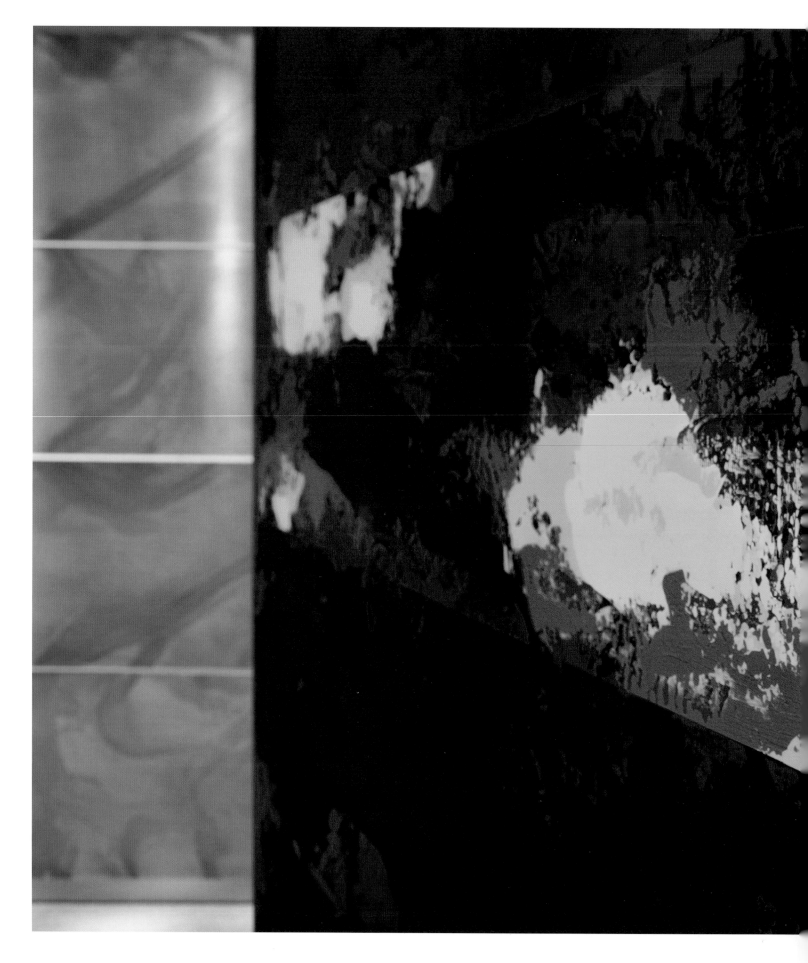

Aspire
London, 1998

*Colour Concept
Signage
Paintings
Poster*

37

Aspire is an organization that helps the spinally injured.

The main treatment centre for the London area is the National Training Centre in Stanmore, Middlesex.

Between 1995-1998 Foster + Partners designed and built an annexe with a theatre and dance studio, a large swimming pool and a learning centre.

Here, in the dance studio, a group of severely disabled patients exercise and perform.

Here, in the pool, the patients and their families swim and play.

Here, within the main floor, in full Foster transparency, seriously injured and disabled people build up the computer skills that enable them to get on with the rest of their lives.

Water and light and above all a sense of optimism are visually built in to the architecture of the centre, so as to invest the new building with an active, living core.

And then a few colour accents signal this liveliness.

A bright yellow stresses the sunlight above the rippling water of the pool.

The hall is also open to residents from the area.

The patients, many of them very young, are in every sense amidst life here.

A crucial difficulty, almost an impossibility, in talking about the contribution of colour to a building, is usually the quite banal factor of the size of the building.

And when it comes to Foster + Partners, the buildings can be of a quite considerable size.

But it is really quite logical: the colours are clearly part of a much larger context that cannot be reproduced or explained or captured by even the most advanced digital cameras.

I add an accent and can show an accent, but in the nature of things I cannot show the 100-metre long, bright white corridor that leads to the very blue door.

I show the blue door! But I also show my awareness of the problem by playing the music without breaks, so to speak. Only as a series of noisy drumbeats!

These images from a very real world can only show a version of real life.

THE ASPIRE NATIONAL TRAINING CENTRE

Reichstag
Berlin, 1999

Colour Concept

45

46 The German Reichstag building in Berlin unfolds as a dramatically concentrated history of modern Germany.

From the darkness of hopeless insanity to the bright hope of frail democracy. In an accumulation of bricks and symbols and spaces and corridors, symmetry and hierarchy and layer upon layer, the most symbolic city's most symbolic centre.

Foster's bright, transparent ceiling for this incarnation has already been described in detail.

In 1996 when I was invited on board the project, several deliberations about the colour scheme were already in play.

But the addition of a series of strictly functional acoustic panels in the long row of large meeting rooms cried out for more colours and thus at the same time for more of a system.

A layered, horizontal division of the building's colour accents was sketched out, and a dazzling blue was proposed for the seats in the plenary assembly hall.

A massively powerful colour element against the discreet background of natural stone and a scale of carefully matched grey shades on walls, floors and tables.

The requirements of TV transmissions were a very strong factor here. The lighting is not just the lighting of the space, but also of the space as TV studio. The medium sets the tone!

Nothing must flicker or jump in the eye of the viewer!

The vertical colour idiom of the building gave each floor a colour that glinted sporadically on the doors and panelling of the great stone colossus. A yellow floor, a blue one, a dark red one, etc.

The horizontal 'colour carousel' dances through an excitable scale of 12 clear colours, randomly distributed in club and meeting rooms.

Three clear blues, a deep red, a discreet green and two bright yellows. A grey for the red doors.

A 'meaningless' medley that is not meant to be interpreted; a friendly embrace of the spaces with the strongly colour-saturated acoustic panels' functional, potent surfaces.

The building contains a number of crucial clashes: The fragments of the ruins (preserved) meet the shiny new building.

Old history meets new history.

Graffiti (the Cyrillic greetings of the Soviet liberation troops) meet freshly polished glass areas.

Steel meets stone.

The transparent meets the massively solid; and with this of course, the strong accents of the colours and their mutual encounters that sparkle in the stone masses of the very large building.

Christo and Jean-Claude wrapped the Reichstag. Foster unwrapped it and let it blossom as a huge, functional, very inviting building.

Gerhard Richter's large Hinterglas painting (6)
peeps out with coquettish asymmetry through the
facade windows like an unintentional warning
of some of the colours that the great building has
swallowed, digested and made its own.

No colour in the building is to be interpreted,
no colour can be interpreted, and no colour must
be interpreted.
The next colour must strike the eye with such
appropriate closeness and quickness that we
eliminate the trap of interpretation.
Here colours are just colours. This contribution to
the life of the building must also breathe freely.

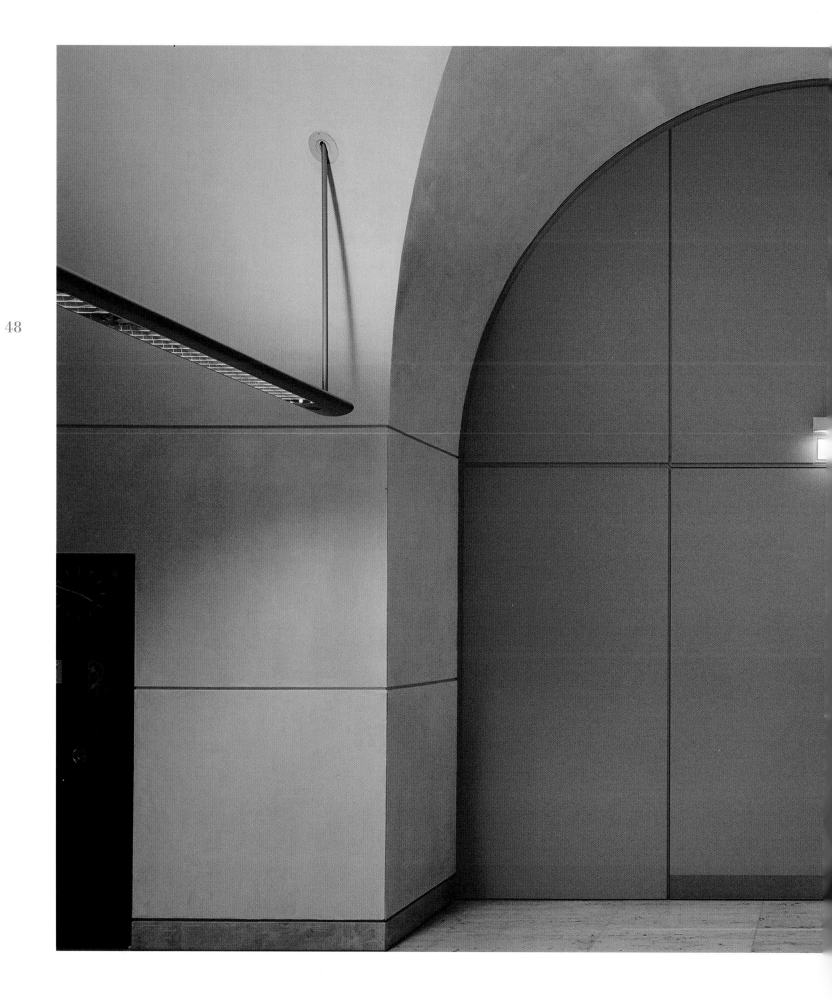

> *I invited Per Arnoldi, a distinguished graphic artist based in Copenhagen, to join the design team. Per and I have worked together on many projects in the past – including the Commerzbank in Frankfurt, and more recently the Biomedical Sciences Building for Imperial College in London – with an exceptional degree of shared succes. For the Reichstag we devised a family of twelve strong colours, running through the spectrum: one room might be a deep French blue, another sunflower yellow, or a brilliant red and so on. We presented these ideas to the Building Committee on a freezing March morning in 1998, on site at the Reichstag. Colours inevitably carry political overtones and I was afraid that we might become mired in an endless debate about which were acceptable. But Per was tremendous. Together with his combination of passion and logic, the fact that he was able to adress the Committee in German proved critical. At the end of his presentation, everyone applauded! We had our approval.*

Norman Foster in "Rebuilding the Reichstag" 2000

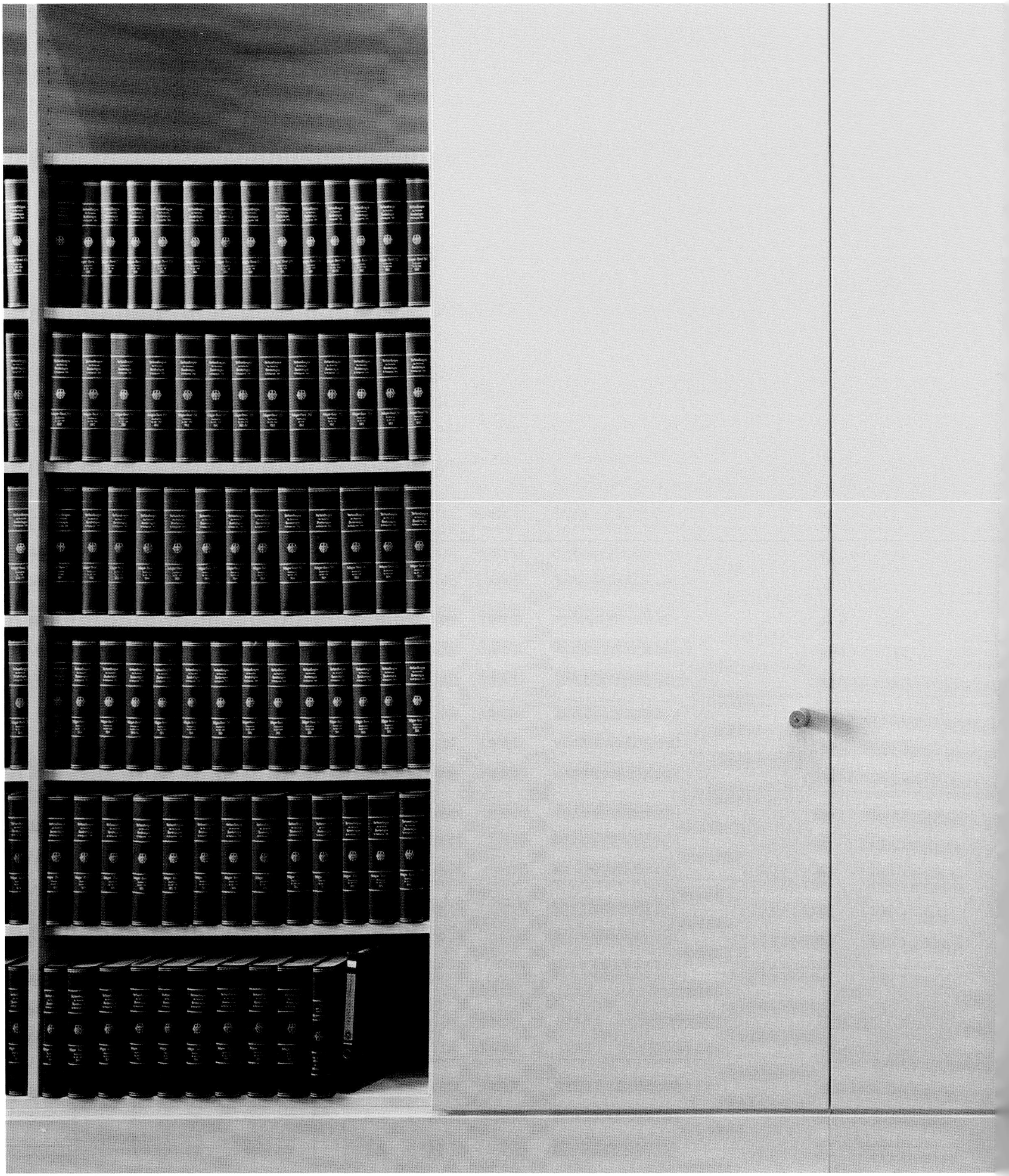

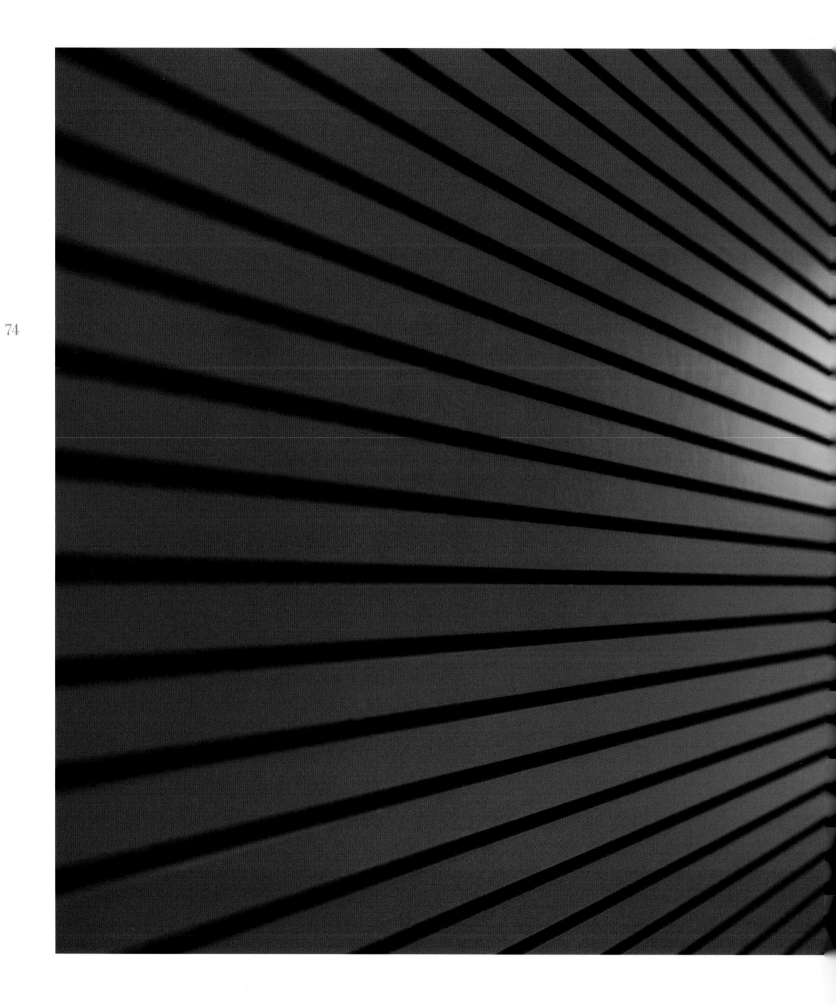

Behind the receptionists in the large bright foyer at the bottom of the World Port Centre's 48-storey round, sparkling tower on the Wilhelmina Pier in Rotterdam's enormous harbour stands a solid reinforced glass plate.
It stops the draught and carries the Centre's identifying text.
Behind it, the wall is expressed in so light a grey that it could easily be a shadow. But it is there.
On these light grey walls two paintings were supposed to sum up the rigorous asceticism and throbbing dynamism of the building.

I chose to paint directly on the glass plates, which I would then have floating out from the wall, like a much-reworked replica of the transparent nakedness of the bottom layer of glass.

Unfortunately safety considerations – as we understood it, having finished with the many layers behind the glass – would not permit these to be hung, hovering, with no frames.
But that is life – now and then in real life...

Hinterglasmalerei – reverse glass painting – is an ancient discipline.
Fascinating, because it constantly fixes the stroke and closes it in with the next stoke. You cannot get in and correct anything at all.
You have to begin with the 'foreground' and end by painting the background. And there is no way back to the start.
You finish painting, and then you turn the glass around.
What you get is what you get!
Of course, it is easier with the big splashes and those gestures that automatically leave their mark – if you are on form, that is.
For no-regrets also requires precision work, even if it represents nothing but itself.
You cannot make a bold stroke without boldness.
You cannot hesitate in mid-motion without killing it.
You cannot paint fast slowly.

During the process, chance events of such great beauty and striking finality take place so that you are constantly tempted to doubt the anticpated goal and change direction and follow this newborn path in blind enthusiasm.
Many painters have lived by letting this happen.

When evening fell after the last day of painting, and the four large painted glass plates had been given a last layer of dark blue and stood there drying, ready for a nerve-wrackingly risky hanging, the installation was more beautiful than ever.
True, they got in the way of all the people moving through the foyer the next morning, but the big razor-sharp smouldering blue glass plates so nonchalantly placed in the lit foyer kept me floating blissfully along ... one fine night in Rotterdam.

World Port Center

Port of Rotterdam

Gemeentelijke Brandweer Rotterdam / RHRR

Politie Rotterdam - Rijnmond

ENECO Energie

The Alexander Fleming Building

Colour Concept
Signage

94 'See it as a big canvas,' was Norman's invitation to do the colour scheme of the five-storey back wall of the Alexander Fleming Building in 1994.

The wall itself was seen through a series of load-bearing columns at the front edge of the balcony, which more or less subdivided it into 12 sections. At the same time the soft overhead light from the atrium ceiling cast a moving and mobile network of shadows on the wall.

I selected a sequence of colours from bright yellow to orange and used the divisions of the columns to demarcate the colour scheme.

The progression went from the brightest colour up in the light to the darkest colour down in the gloom at the bottom of the hall.

That was of course one decision – where I would intensify the light, and where the darkness would be invited in.

The opposite decision, to let the brightest colour brighten up the darkest corner and so to speak reverse the sequence, was also a possibility.

But in this formidably top-lit large space it was rather tempting to challenge the darkness – that is, to tone it down, down into orange, down into the bottom right-hand corner, down into the glowing, smouldering twilight bonfire that appears when the sunlight retreats at the end of the day.

The columns divide up the back wall, but at the same time in the changing light of the day they cast an infinitely varied network of shadows on the back wall, where the colours of the yellow scale meet the shadows, and in the process obscure and confound our experience of the sequence.

Is it two yellows that meet or is it a passing shadow of the same colour?

The space and the light paint over my painting.

At the opposite, northern end of the space, a strong ultramarine similarly runs from the lowest darkness to the uppermost five bright storeys.

The signposting at the blue end matches the blue.

The wall of the lift shafts matches the orange sequence.

The painting coheres.

Sir Alexander Fleming Building

Computer Teaching Laboratories →

Multidisciplinary Laboratories

Lifts

Disabled Toilets ♿

Telephones ←

The Flowers Building
2001

Colour Concept
Signage
Painting

The Alexander Fleming Building was the large
(and first) canvas ... the Flowers Building,
alongside it, is a second little gem.
Rigorously arranged, simply formulated, its built-in
divisions gave the job structure.
The end wall of the foyer was just asking for
an art-work, a story told. A dramatic meeting with
some of the scientists who were to work in this
building marked out the subjects.
In Danish, when we have to choose between a rock
and a hard place, we say 'it's a choice between
plague and cholera'.
A dynamic row of microscopic narratives about the
visually fascinating development of the diseases
was my material.
Cholera won.

“ *This is a battlescene.*
A cholera virus is attacking and actually invading
a healthy red blood cell, hibernating, threatening
and finally, bursting out, destroying the cell...
In the good old manner of the master of
spectacular battles and dramatic events, I have
used a Rubenesque diagonal to tell the story
as dramatically as possible. Disguised in beautiful
colours, this is a battle of life and death!

115

Faculty Building
2004

Colour Concept
Signage
Paintings

118   Within a backyard, hidden and forgotten, surrounded by sad dying trees and a cramped car park in the middle of Imperial College's green and friendly campus, there was room.

The Faculty's new administration building could be erected here, and, as it turned out when Foster went to work on the plan, it was also here where the perfect passage lines of human movement intersected.

Now accessible and usable.

This diagonal section cuts sharply through the new building's glass body.

Now, as the darkness of the backyard emerged into the light, Foster rightly thought that this building should be highlighted, all the way up into the clouds, with a richly varied play of colours. I hung on to the 'play', but let it reveal itself in three hues of blue.

An analysis of the motion and intensity of the sun on the building in the course of the day gave us the code for the placing of the blue and the transparent facade elements.

The dramatic diagonal section was delimited and marked by a row of flaming orange columns.

A dark blackish-blue created a calm interior just around the technical core.

The steel produced clear highlights.

Blue and strongly 'wrapped', this central building linked our approaches to four buildings for Imperial College closely together.

> The sun analysis also gave us the starting-point
> for the stained glass of the four storeys.
> From the dark bottom of the ground floor to
> the bright yellow of the top floor.
> An old trick ... but it appears to work.

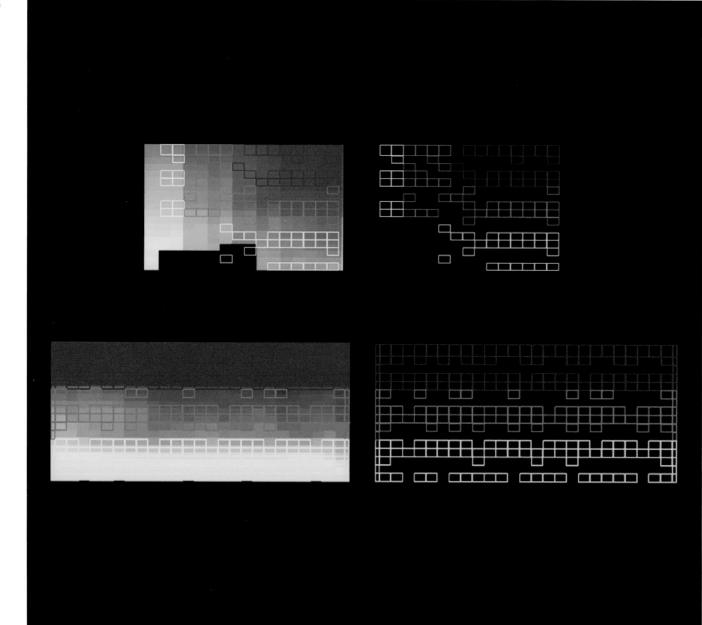

Tanaka Business School
2004

Colour Concept
Painting
(Hoarding)

The building of the extension of the Tanaka Business School along Exhibition Road created at the same time a main entrance for Imperial College as a whole.

The large back wall called for a colour and a symbol.

This would have been the obvious place for a heraldic device – a crest.

The traditional wall.

The management were adamant that this was not to the way they wanted to go.

It would have been meaningless to let the bold, soaringly light building take a giant step forward and then drag it back with a traditional decorative approach.

So what then?

The colour was straightforward enough.

A dark blue with the grey and the white.

A silver corridor to the inner courtyard where the Faculty Building's scale in the same blue would remind the eye ... and the brain.

And the image, the motif: an intensely coloured brain scan.

Laid flat (which given its scientific incorrectness turned out to be the greatest hurdle) and intensely coloured.

A yellow/orange sequence from the Alexander Fleming and Flowers buildings hovering within Tanaka's steel/blue space.

Professor Joe Hainal won the argument about the unscientific placing of the brain for me and supplied us with a perfect scan – of his own brain. This emerged at the inauguration when, directly asked by the Queen, he had to reveal the 'secret of the origin'.

The grey shades were then manually and randomly translated into the optimum play of colours, which transformed the now totally brainless brain into a symbol.

A symbol of the brain the students 'had better bring along' and the brain-power Imperial College possesses.

Bring us your brain and we will fill it ... was my working title.

It had to lie down to fill the space.

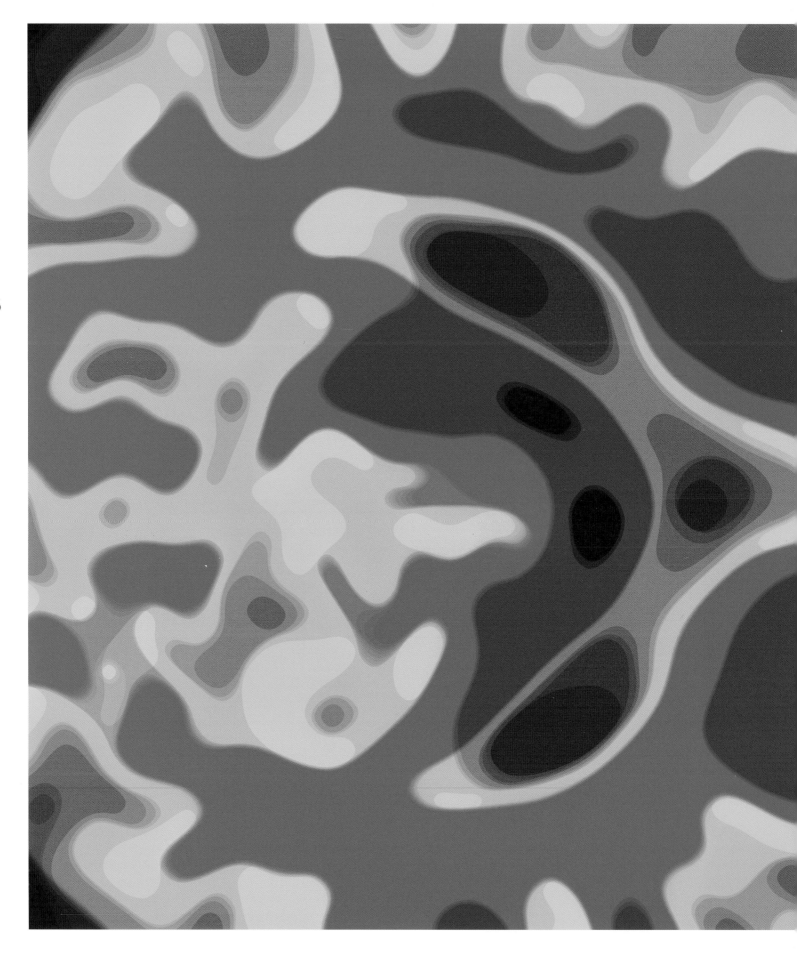

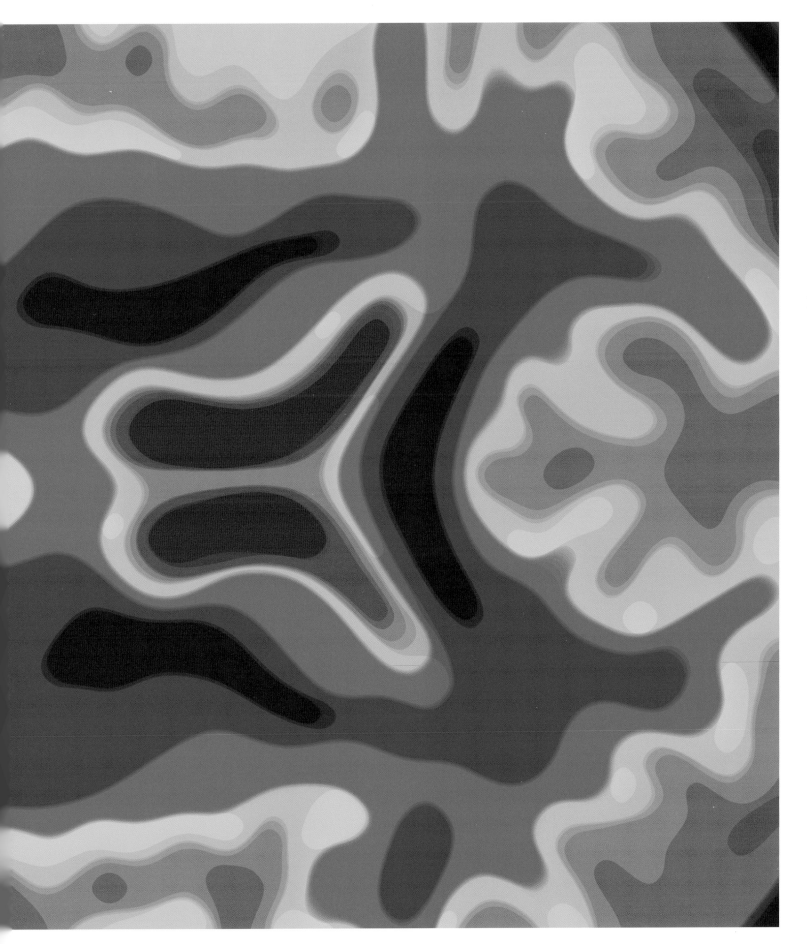

The National
Police Monument
The Mall
London, 2005

*Concept
Graphic Design*

141

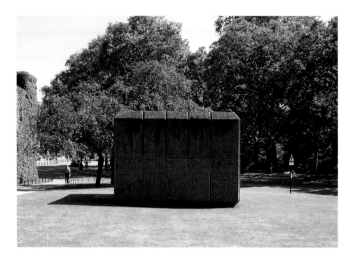

142 The National Police Memorial Trust was established after the murder of WPC Yvonne Fletcher in 1984.
With the continued setting-up of memorial plaques to fallen officers, the need grew for an overall national monument to these tragic losses.
A site was chosen and a long, laborious process could begin.
At the east end of the Mall, in front of the Admiralty, a small triangular lawn lived its own unheeded life. This was to be the place.
The area by the Mall and Horse Guard Parade is strewn with monuments, all to wars and battles, fought and finished, won or lost. But over.
And now a monument was to be added which, unlike the other powerful reminders, was a memorial to an ongoing battle, never to be won.
An open, endless monument, so to speak.
The lawn was occupied by an uncommonly ugly, large, dominant and apparently unbudgeable Underground air vent. Exhaust-stained worn concrete with a small door set within it.

Spencer de Grey took me past the project during a visit to the design office, with an explicit warning that I was to advise but otherwise not to be involved.
But projects have their own inertia and that was not how it went.
The concrete block had begun to grow. With every attempt to hide it, it swelled like wet oats.

All sculptural camouflage just increased the overall volume, however artistically unquadratic it looked.
Other tricks had to be tried.
To draw attention away from an object, as all conjurors know, you have to direct attention to something else. Shift the focus.
To reduce the concrete block to B, we had to create an A.
That was the exercise!
In a small pond we erected a shining, illuminated glass column.
A straight A to ace out the bulky B of the block.
Something light to counter something heavy.
Something transparent against something solid.
And the massive body of the concrete block, door and all, was clad in black marble and a flaming red creeper.

In the gable of the seriously black block, behind glass, lies a book in which the names of all the fallen officers have been inscribed, and continue to be inscribed in the event of death in the line of duty.

The semi-transparent glass block in the small pond is lit up in the darkness by a vibrant blue in memory of the blue lamp that formerly signified the location of a police station.

A limited palette for a very sad story.

99 *The memorial, praised by the judges*
for achieving a sense of 'calm introspection',
was said to be successful as a memorial
'for evoking a sense of past and future,
sadness and pride'.

From Foster+Partners press release, announcing
the Royal Institute of British Architects Award, 2006

149

HM Treasury
London, 2002

Colour Concept
Signage
Paintings
Banners

151

152 In a large generous sweeping (and slightly moving) gesture, a rainbow of suspended banners and a large wall-piece fill the now covered inner courtyards of the rebuilt HM Treasury in London.
The system is quite simple: the banners hang in the ever-changing light five at a time.
Four red and one joker – an orange, in one of the courtyards.
Next space, the joker takes over: four orange and one yellow.
Then four yellow and one bright blue, etc, until the full circle ends in the static 'sum of' the colours on the back wall of the large and very, very tall lobby.
Three yellow, three red, three blue.
The play of light makes the small differences appear and disappear in constant movement.
The banners form a discreet and slightly transparent Mondrianesque installation within the enormous building, seen from inside as a new colour-filled out/inside.
The rest is white and a very blue carpet.
Metallic signage, all quite cool.
New wall pieces along the perimeter of the building all shine a bright yellow and draw the daylight into the room.
After its remake, the former dark labyrinths of this building have disappeared into a lot of light.

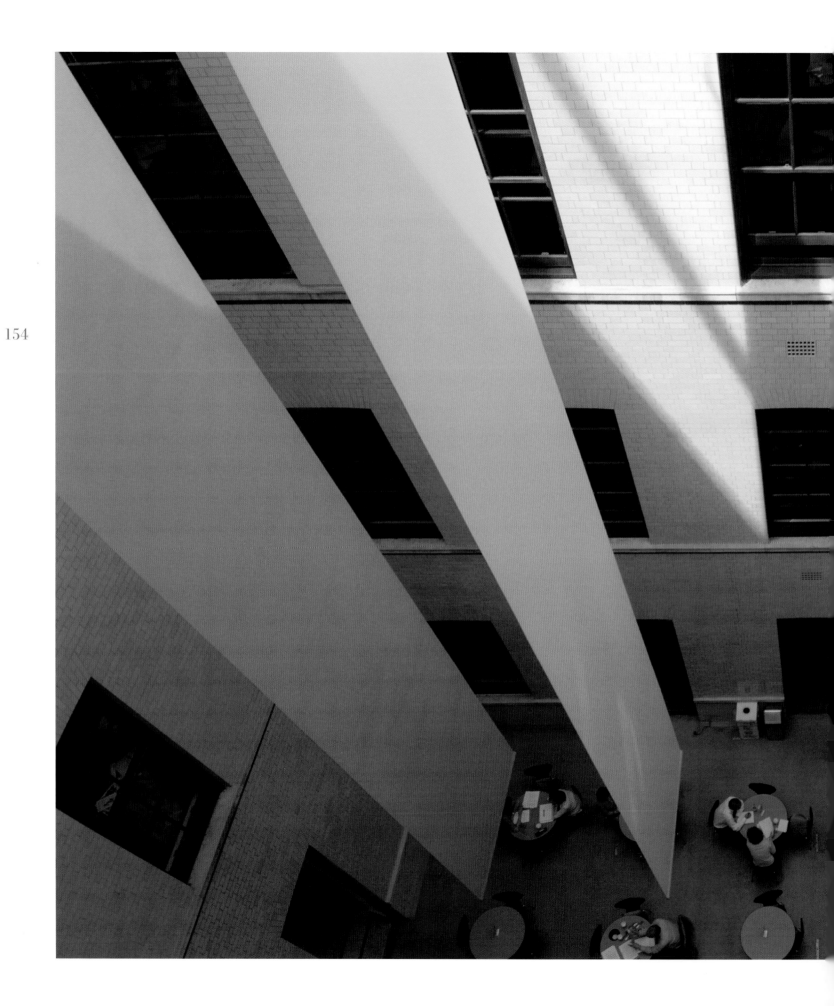

155

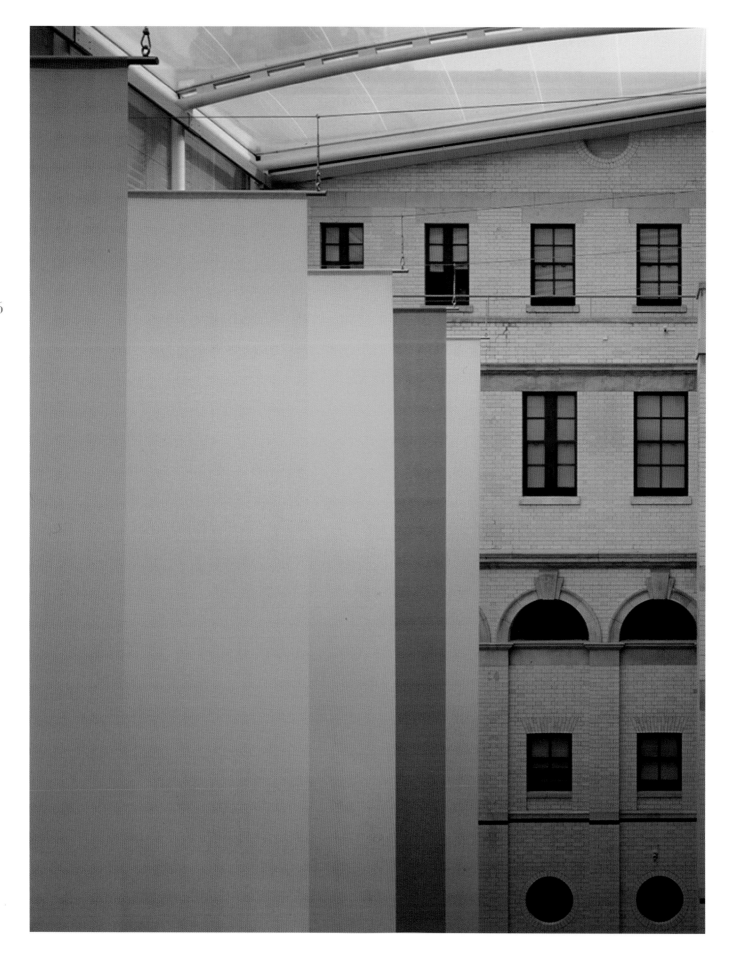

*" New wall pieces along the perimeter of
the building all shine a bright yellow and draw
the daylight into the room.*

164

Trafalgar Square
(World Squares for All)
Cafe and Public Toilets
London, 2003

Colour Concept

171

172 The generous and radical reorganisation of Trafalgar Square as the first part of the larger World Squares project created a sunny, peaceful, safe pedestrian area from the steps of the National Gallery down to Nelson and his lions.

Into the plinth, on both sides of a broad stretch of stairs, public toilets (left) and a café space (right) were excavated and then introduced.

The ceilings are quite low.

Within the ocean of toilet-steel, a strong red is introduced; while a dense back-painted bright yellow glass wall added one sparkling accent to the cafe's uniform white.

The trick is to use one colour and make it perform with the power of a thousand.

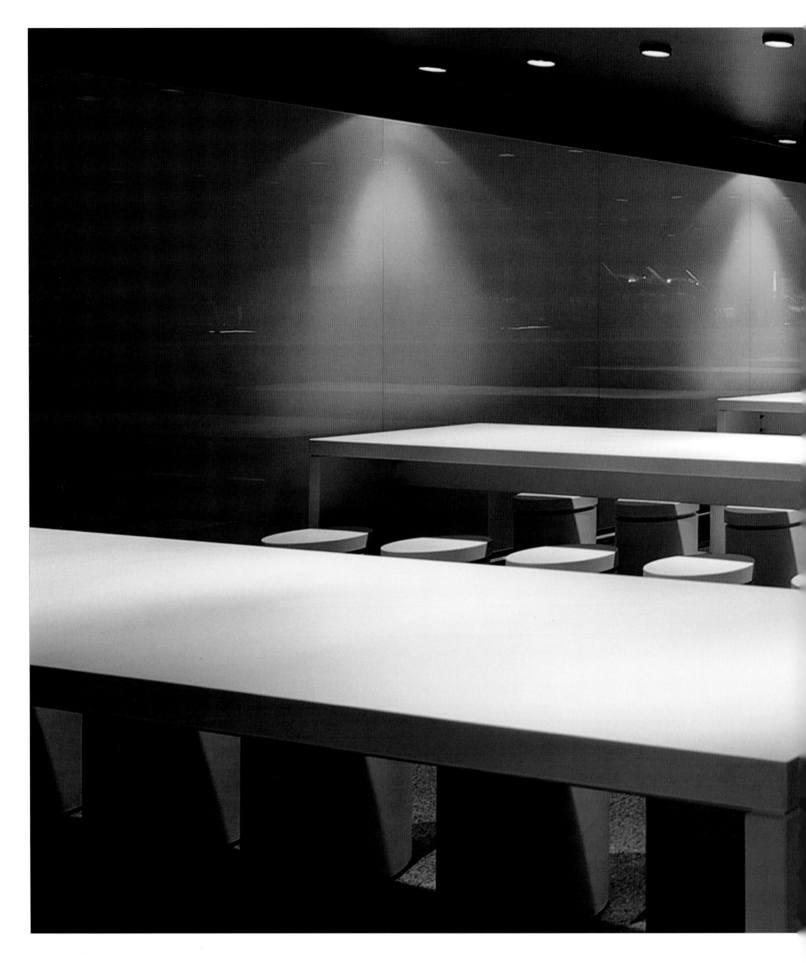

The Congress Center
Valencia, 1998

Posters

177

This is how the building with its iconic canopy and elegantly curved brise-soleil has to function: between the devilish heat of the days and the breezy cool of the nights. I thought the poster commissioned for the inauguration of this conference centre, the Palacio de Congresos in Valencia, should be TWO posters – one a warm day poster with the cool building and the other its opposite, a nocturnal version with a glowing warm facade.

There was a magic moment at the inauguration in 1998 when we stepped out of the building into the early evening.

The sun was just still up and the remainder of a very warm day lingered in the air.

On the other side of the building the moon had appeared and was already signalling the cool of the night.

The twin posters, which had been up all over town announcing, or rather celebrating, the occasion for a week, were for real.

I did not, however, expect them to be that prescient.

Design is luck!

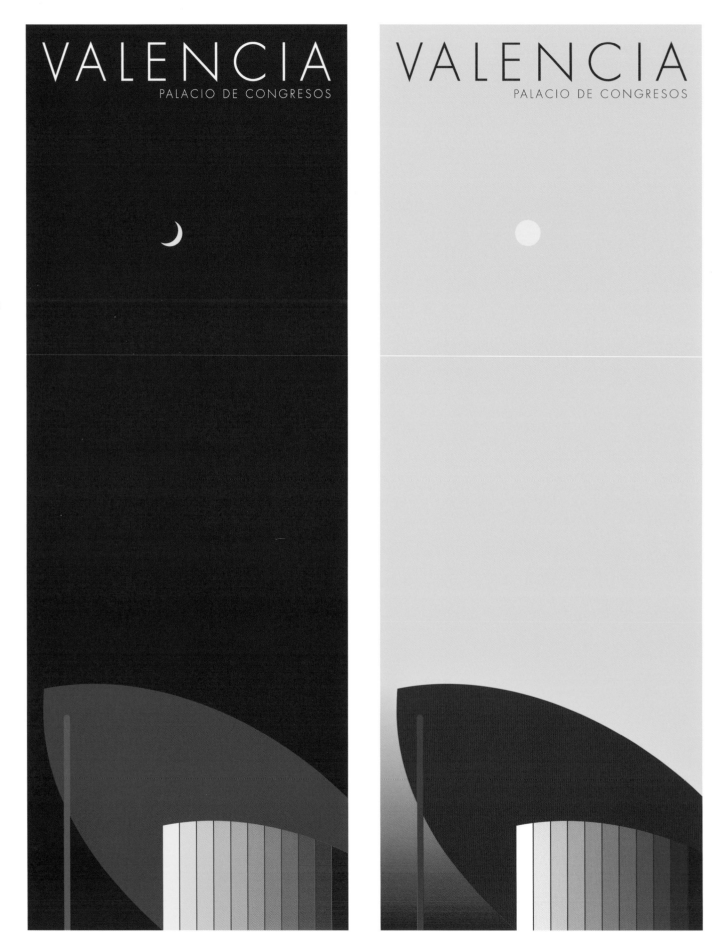

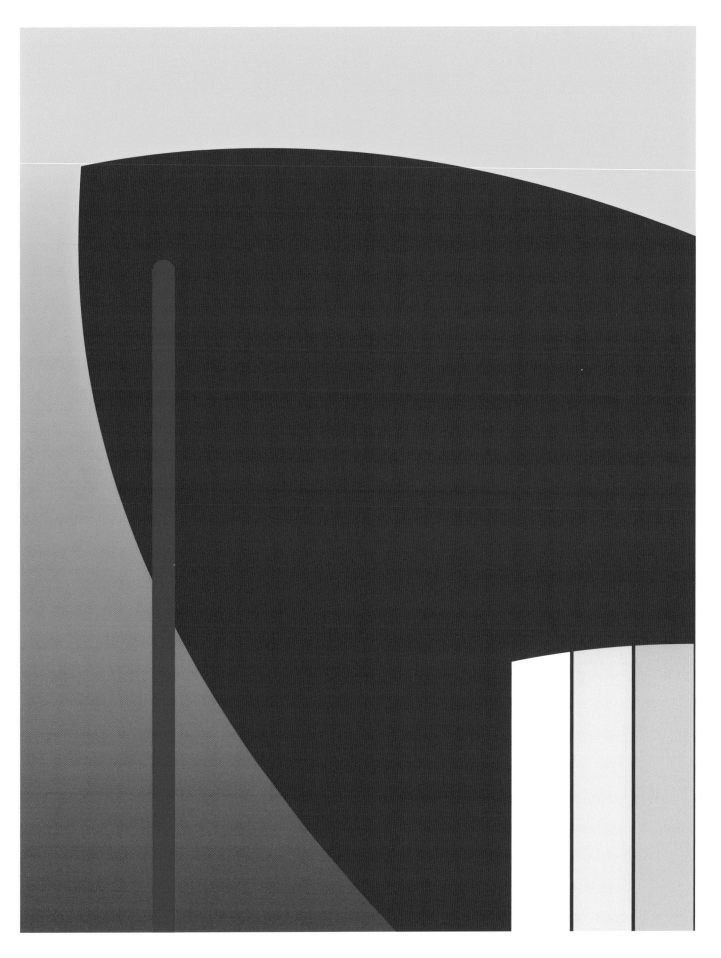

The Norman Foster Studio:
Exploring the City

Sainsbury Center for Visual Arts
Norfolk, 2000

Exhibition Design
Graphic Design

Variations on a theme: a series of exhibitions
– *The Norman Foster Studio - Exploring the City,
2000; The Foster Studio - Exploring the City, 2001;
Norman Foster - The Architect's Studio, 2001* have
all been working hard to demonstrate and
communicate the myriad of efforts, the endless trial
and errors, the high hopes and the proper and
practical solutions which inevitably go into every
architectural project, both very large and very
small.
To make sense of this, to organise this chaos and
show it the way towards some kind of order and
buildable structure is almost impossible.
Whatever you use – the most immaculate models,
the sharpest photos and screens, the most articulate
graphics and elaborate storylines, the first sketches
and the latest mock-ups – it will always be far
more elegant and neat and safe than the real life
which is the real life of this office.
This is the task: to tell the story without the details
and without loosing the feel of the details at the
same time.
To trim it without killing it.
To show final results and keep the utopian feeling
and spirit of both the place and the office.
Architecture operates in real life.
Outside.
The exhibitions must tell this story with all the
flavour of real life inside.
This is tricky.

"If the spaces we create do not move the heart and mind, then they are surely only addressing one part of their function."

Norman Foster

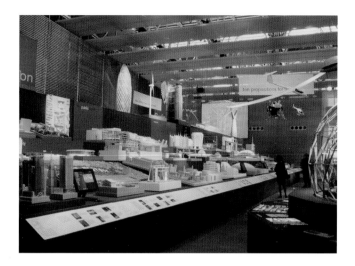

The Norman Foster Studio:
Exploring the City

The British Museum
London, 2001

Graphic Design

Norman Foster:
The Architect's Studio

Louisiana Museum of Modern Art
Copenhagen, 2001

Exhibition Design
Graphic Design
Posters

188 The illusion was almost too perfect.
The large exhibition space at the Louisiana
Museum of Modern Art north of Copenhagen was
the chosen location.
In 2001, work from the Foster studio filled a
balcony the full width of the room at one end.
When the large floor-to-ceiling print showing the
view from the London office out over the Thames
went up on the opposite wall you almost felt as
if you were there.
The long exhibition benches replicated the long
tables of the office, the view down the view down,
and the myriad of models and sketches told in
almost 1:1 scale the story of the bustling
workplace.
An exhibition has to be organised, structured;
articulate, readable and easily understood.
The clutter and the mess and the thousands of
movements, the criss-crossing lines of communication of the everyday workplace are almost
unreproducable.
The layout of the room did the trick!

NORMAN **FOSTER**

Arkitekturens værksteder 8.9. – 9.12. 2001

Swiss Re London

LOUISIANA

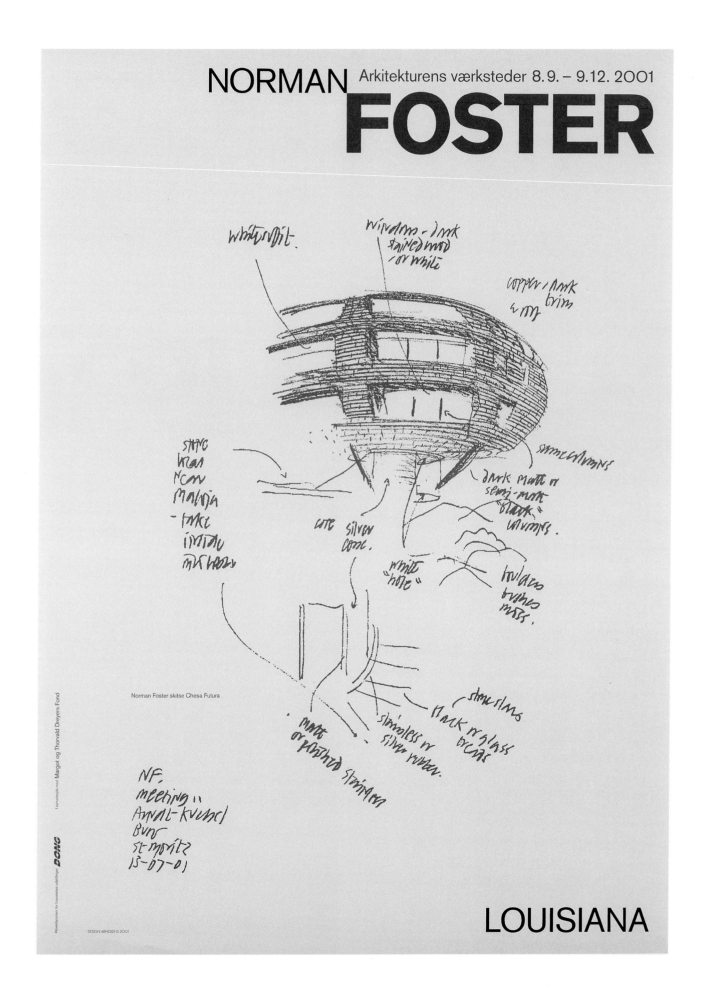

Norman Foster skitse Chesa Futura

Modern Britain 1929-1939

The Design Museum
London, 1998

Exhibition Design
Graphic Design

192 The main room was always our main problem when, as a small anxious group, we struggled with the basic layout for the exhibition: Modern Britain 1929-1939 at the Design Museum in London in 1998. Columns! The room had two rows of very solid columns which would not go away. We tried to ignore them, attack them, camouflage them or hide them. They stayed very still and even seemed to grow on plan.
Norman passed the small round table by the tall window of the office towards the river and stopped!
Panic! I mean, we had nothing to show him but frustration and dead-end solutions.
Norman grabbed a pencil, looked at the plan and drew a curved, snakelike unbroken line curling and folding around the columns.
'Something like that?' he said and was off.
The columns were now totally integrated, high-lighted and hidden at the same time; the curved strip of wall dramatically entertaining and now long enough to allow for the rich story of the exhibition to unfold.
Cut-outs in the wall could naturally allow the more fragile objects to be seen, while the protru-ding surface let the images and long-running two story-lines get closer to the visitor.
All in the very style of the period in question.
It looked easy!

198 The Jubilee Line extension culminates with the impressive Canary Wharf Station.
A poster commissioned to celebrate the inauguration of the new station was also a tribute to architect Roland Paoletti, who took the initiative and saw the whole design-project through from the deepest shaft to the glassy outburst overground.
I know I exaggerated the depth a bit to get the feel of this fantastic match between the deep dark bottom and the light transparent top.
The logo for the London Underground is one of the best designs in the world.
In Foster + Partners station it is utilized generously up there ... and down under, on my poster, where it really runs, it tells the whole connecting story in one elegant stroke ... of luck.

202 Along the Great West Road out of London, a few Art Deco industrial buildings have survived in all their streamlined, ship-shape, optimistic glamour.

JCDecaux lives at no. 991, a white whale from 1936.

Foster + Partners have hollowed out and built-in and perfected the whole complex, and with a single great wing-sweep have covered a demonstration street for JCDecaux's street furniture between the annexe and the pre-war main building.

The imposing, tall glass section of the vestibule sheds light on the two murals inside: a very tall version of my first New York poster for JCDecaux, and opposite, a London motif with Nelson very high up on his column within Foster's World Squares.

This was where it all began.

This is where it all hangs together.

Very red and very blue.

205

Morelondon
London, 2003

Feature Walls
Graphic Design
Colour Concept

207

Morelondon is a large ten-storey office building on the developing site next to Tower Bridge and Foster + Partners spacey home for the Greater London Authority.

Most of the ingredients were already in place when I was asked to join the project.

This was – or rather, as we go to press, this is – the task: to visually entertain on the two 8 x 14 metre entrance walls a wide range of kinetic possibilities, and to indicate the number of the building – a clear but also intriguing '3'.

I reduced the number of proposed colours to one and cut a large Helvetica '3' (the typeface had already been decided) out of the same indigo blue. Delicately the shadows of the cut-out make it readable in subtle tones, and at the same time rather rough and direct, as of course the cut-out reveals what is behind: bits and pieces of the construction grid.

Towards the other end of the walls, both layers of blue move within a vertical grid, allowing daylight to reach into the rooms inside. One number, one colour, two layers. I could not reduce it any further.

The movement of light and shadow will do the rest.

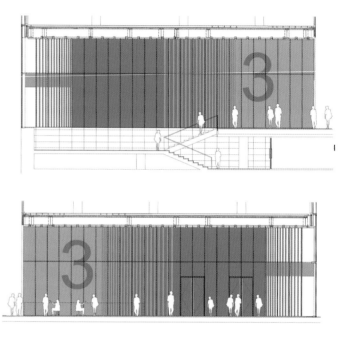

Norman Foster Works 1-6

*Graphic Concept
with Thomas Manns*

214 The work on the six volumes of 'complete works' of Norman Foster started in 1999.
The sheer volume of projects is impressive. And the consistency of their quality is almost scary. How has this enormous body of work maintained such quality for more than 45 years?
Even more scary was the task of condensing and communicating the structure, the grid and the strong inner vision of one man and his hundreds and hundreds of helpers.
Norman once talked about reaching the end of a building project only to turn around to check whether the beginning, the fire of the first idea and original vision, was still alive and present in the final result?
This has also been the challenge of the six (so far) volumes, 4 of which have been published – to make a construction which could carry the story forward, allowing it to breathe and jump freely and naturally backward and forward.
These backward jumps, especially, turned out to be very intriguing. They suggested, in their 'retro-movements' the possibility of uncovering some resonant connective tissue in the work.
This in itself developed the basic grid even further. I have always believed that solutions come from within the subject and the challenges at hand; that the order and articulation, which is such a strong and beautiful part of the work of this amazing office, come from the very core of the job – from

digging and distilling rather than high-flying for some heavenly, outer-space inspiration.
A wide range of colours for the binding was researched but in the end, again, after peacocking around a strong palette, an inbuilt, so to say, steely metal grey was chosen, communicating the balance between the solid and the transparent which has been the signature force of this office.

Norman Foster Works

Foster Works 2

Foster Works 2

Foster Works 1

Projects for Computer Technology
1969–1971

In the late 1960s Computer Technology
was a rapidly expanding young company
– the first in Britain to make microchips.
Our first project was the conversion of
an old canning factory on an incredibly
tight budget. We built furniture from
white melamine panels bolted together;
we cut the legs off standard plastic seat
and bent them to create easy chairs; w
carpeted the whole building; and in
process we transformed social hab
Previously people flicked solder
the floor, because it was dirty;
longer – we had created a sp
they took pride. We were in
of designing a new buildi
when unexpected planni
made temporary accor
a priority – office sp
employees was re
weeks. The solut
structure – a p
– which was
and lasted

Berliners have a great deal of pride in, and a great fondness for, their new Reichstag – and I've grown used to encountering the building in some fairly unexpected guises! David Nelson, in conversation with the editor, 2002
Left: A small cast-metal model of the Reichstag, sold as a souvenir of Berlin and collected by David Nelson.
Right: A chocolate bar, featuring the Reichstag in relief, was produced by the German confectionery company Rausch and presented to members of the Bundestag and the Foster team to mark the official opening of the building. This example, owned by David Nelson, is one of the few to have survived.

For me the only true test of a public building is the degree to which the public accepts it. So it is very rewarding to discover that three-and-a-half million people queue to visit the Reichstag every year.

Norman Foster

Foster on Foster

*Graphic Concept
with Thomas Manns*

218 Only a strong glowing colour could match the density of this little compact book and its hightech outfit.
A luminous orange – red carrying strong bits of the rich text as quotes.
Again, the choice of colour is made as simple as possible.
One warm accent in Foster + Partners' silvery, magically metallic world.

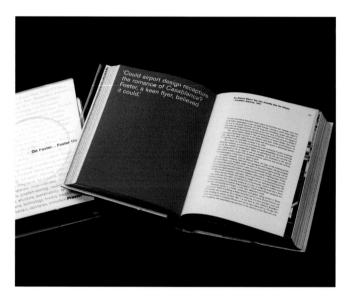

On Foster... Foster On

'Could airp...
the romance o...
Foster', a keen fl...
it could'.

The Lignacite Lecture
London, 2006

Poster
Graphic Design

Graphic design and visual communication
often relies on jokes.
The arrow pointing downwards and reading: up,
you know.
Some new, some old, some good, some not so
good or even worse.
The annual Lignacite seminar and lecture 2006,
coinciding with the publication of this book, took
place September 27 in the new Tanaka building
on Exhibition Road in London.
Title of the evening the title of the book.
David Nelson was invited to talk about art and
architecture and colour and selected experiences
from our 10 years of collaboration. Prominently
among the results the Tanaka Building. My poster
announcing the evening is a joke, playing on
the balance between what we read and what we
se and what we understand and how we percieve
colours and non-colours.
A poster is supposed to catch your attention,
confuse and entertain your senses, fill your imagi-
nation with the seen and the unseen and the
in between, wet your appetite and get you there.

This not a pipe, Magritte, this is a poster.

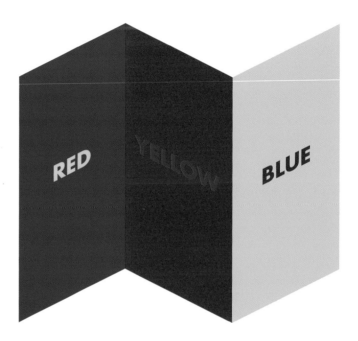

221

LIGNACITE LECTURE 2006 · ART + ARCHITECTURE : **COLOUR IS COMMUNICATION** · AN EVENING WITH **PER ARNOLDI**, ARTIST/DESIGNER AND **DAVID NELSON**, FOSTER + PARTNERS
TANAKA BUSINESS SCHOOL · **SEPTEMBER 27 2006** · **18.30 PM** · IMPERIAL COLLEGE · EXHIBITION ROAD · SOUTH KENSINGTON · LONDON SW7 2AZ

EPILOGUE

Hemingway's old trick from the preface to the splendidly sentimental Parisian memoir *A Moveable Feast* seems appropriate.
He reels off all the things he cannot include, but then – hocus pocus! – includes them anyway.
That might be useful here, where it is impossible to finish without thinking about the projects that, for one reason or another, were not realised.
The money ran out ... time ran out! ... the scaffolding had been taken down when we had to climb it ... I had misunderstood the client's briefing...

So nothing came of the colours around the formidable spiral ramp in the middle of the new library of the London School of Economics, although the wall-sized triple radiators of the ground floor would have been just the thing for my three-yellow, three-red, three-blue solution, and the incredibly generous skylight would have bathed all the colours in 24-hour natural light.

And nothing came of the big internal blue box that was to house LIFFE's testosterone-fuelled activities in which the many hundreds of young traders were to wage war over futures and options on an incalculably vast battlefield of a column-free trading floor on the big building site at Spitalfields in the City of London.

At the back entrance to More London's building no. 3 in Tooley Street we struggled for a long time with a marker, a steel sculpture that would give motoring guests a landmark to turn off at.

The engineering calculations of the wind load recalled the Faculty Building's splendiferously coloured lighting diagrams, and were constantly more fascinating in their own right than the 8-metre tall twisted-steel thingummy I was working on. And the colour distribution over the 9-floor back wall in the foyer progressed optimistically from a discreetly toned indigo to a self-chosen chaos of colours – without being used.

I think a single red colour in the big concert hall for the Sage in Gateshead was what emerged from the initial discussions, and a number of geometrical totems for the West London Academy had to yield the floor to the desire for more narrative images of dolphins. But that is how it goes with geometry and dolphins.

The poster series for the opulent apartment project in St. Moritz was superfluous before it was printed because the apartments apparently sold themselves; at any rate, they did not have to be advertised as strongly as posters must necessarily – in the nature of the genre – try to do.

Things which do not happen do not appear.
But many of the things which do happen tend to disappear.

Graphics and especially the posters for exhibitions etc. are printed in large quantities ... and do not exist today.
They turn into luxurious garbage or instant antiques!
Some of the material reproduced in this book are re-makes, prototypes of early versions, incorrect recollections.
There is however something pleasant, in a world as rock solid and permanent as architecture, that also fledging and fragile matters matter.
Not all of our decisions are forever.
My wildest dream, a facade in gold louvers on an extension of the Foster office would have set the street ablaze ... and though it would probably have capsized the whole tower, I still think my gigantic steel-triangle on the back-wall of the Commerzbank lobby would have made good sense and caused a lot of technical problems doing so.
The souvenirs for the Millaubridge came very close to a kitchy line without crossing it and in spite of our strong efforts to change the rules of the game of heraldry, the design of a coat of arms for Lord Foster never came to a result.

But nothing is spilt milk.
No exercise is superfluous.
Every articulation sharpens the tools.

Graphic design:
Per Arnoldi with
Janne Hiort, Berit Olsen and Annette Botved

Repro and production planning:
Tom Nybroe

Translation:
James Manley

Research:
Thomas Weaver and Kathryn Tollervey

Cover photo:
Dennis Gilbert

A CIP catalogue record for this book
is available from the Library of Congress,
Washington D.C., USA.

Illustrations © 2007 Norman Foster + Partners,
Per Arnoldi and the photographers

© 2007 Birkhäuser – Publishers for Architecture,
P.O. Box 133, CH-4010 Basel, Switzerland.
Part of Springer Science+Business Media
Publishing Group.

Printed on acid-free paper produced of
chlorine-free pulp. TCF ∞ Printed in Germany

ISBN-13: 978-3-7643-7503-4
ISBN-10: 3-7643-7503-5

9 8 7 6 5 4 3 2 1

Photography:

Richard Bryant	p. 55, 57
Foster + Partners	p. 20, 206/207
Dennis Gilbert	p. 36/37, 44/45, 58/59, 94, 104/105, 198
Jens Honoré	p. 212/213, 215, 216/217, 218, 219
Ian Lambot	p. 18/19
London Aerial Photo Library	p. 92/93
Rudi Meisel	p. 48/49, 50/51, 52/53, 54/55, 57, 59, 60/61, 52/63, 64/65, 66/67, 68/69, 70/71, 72/73, 178
James Morris	p. 100/101, 102, 103
Ali Moshiri	p. 132(2), 133
Jacob Nørløv	p. 81, 82, 83, 84, 85
Rosted	p. 9, 191
Lars Schmidt	p. 21, 22, 23, 24, 25, 26(3), 27, 28(2), 29, 30/31, 32/33, 34/35, 78/79, 86/87, 88, 89, 90/91
Barry Wallis	p. 134/135
Nigel Young	p. 6, 39, 40/41, 42(2), 47, 54, 56, 58(2), 76/77, 80, 86/87, 88, 89, 90/91, 97, 98, 99, 106/107, 109(2), 110/111, 112/113, 114/115, 116, 117, 118, 119, 120/121, 124/125, 128, 129, 131, 138/139, 140/141, 142, 143, 144, 144/145, 146, 147, 148/149, 150/151, 154/155, 158, 159, 160/161, 162, 163, 164, 165, 166, 167, 168, 168/169, 170/171, 174/175, 179(2), 182/183, 185(2), 186/187, 188, 189, 192/193, 193, 194/195, 200/201, 204, 205, 223(2)

www.birkhauser.ch